∧ Top Skills

OC Maths Tests

For Opportunity Class Entry Tests
& Scholarship Tests Preparation

Elyse Methven

Five Senses Education Pty Ltd
2/195 Prospect Highway
Seven Hills 2147
New South Wales
Australia

Methven, Elyse
Top Skills – OC Mathematics Tests
ISBN 978 1 74130 132 8

CONTENTS

How to use this book:

The tests are designed to prepare students for Opportunity Class mathematics tests, helping students to think mathematically and expand their analytical and problem solving skills. However this book can also be used as a more general tool to enhance a student's problem solving and lateral thinking skills.

For the student...

When answering the practice questions, *do not simply guess* the solutions. This will not allow you to broaden your knowledge. Have a ruler, grid book, and even the Internet nearby as tools of reference.

Remember that the questions vary in their degree of difficulty, and some are quite complex. Do not get frustrated if you cannot work out the answer. The questions are designed to test a range of abilities, and students will have strengths and weaknesses in different areas.

Students may time themselves while completing each test. However, it is important not to rush through the tests. Do not sacrifice accuracy for speed. Use the space provided at the end of the book to work carefully through each question. Drawing diagrams and pictorial representations may assist in finding a solution.

The time allocated to answering each question will vary depending on their complexity. Some questions may be answered in a matter of seconds, while others may take a few minutes. The extension problems located towards the end of the book are of a higher degree of difficulty. They have been engineered to challenge the mind and broaden problem solving and lateral thinking skills.

Tips for the exam ~

How to answer multiple choice questions:

- Read through the question very *carefully.*

- Think of a correct answer *before* the alternatives are given to you.

- If you cannot think of the correct answer, try and *eliminate* any answers that are unlikely or misleading.

- Read the four alternatives and choose the *best* or *closest* answer to what you think the question is asking.

- After choosing the best answer, *mark any difficult questions* so that you can come back to them if you have any spare time at the end of the test.

- *Attempt all questions.* You do not get marks taken off for answering a question incorrectly.

Remember to make sure you...

- *Plan and allocate time* for each question. For example, if the test is 1 hour and there are 60 questions- allocate around 1 minute to answering each question.

- *Do not waste too much time* answering any one question. Choose the best answer and go back to it at the end of the test.

- *Never rush.* Even if you think you know the answer immediately, read it through carefully to make sure you fully understand what it is asking.

OC MATHS TEST 1

1. Jean baked 12 cupcakes. His family ate 8 and Jean ate the remainder. Which calculation shows how many cupcakes Jean ate?

   a) $12 \div 8 = 1\frac{1}{2}$

   b) $8 - 12 = -4$

   c) $12 + 8 = 20$

   d) $12 - 8 = 4$

2. Pablo's friends ordered two coffees, a smoothie and a muffin. How much did their order cost altogether?

   a) $11.50

   b) $13.00

   c) $13.50

   d) $14.50

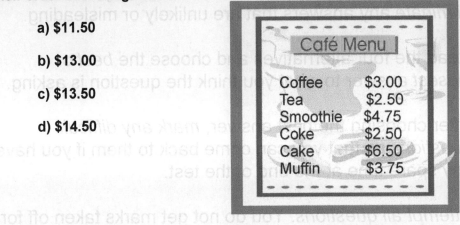

Café Menu

Coffee	$3.00
Tea	$2.50
Smoothie	$4.75
Coke	$2.50
Cake	$6.50
Muffin	$3.75

3. What is 50% of $48?

   a) $24

   b) $12

   c) $4.80

   d) $20

4. Seong paints four rectangular walls. Each wall is 6 metres wide and 4 metres high. If 1 litre of paint is needed for every square metre, how many litres of paint does Seong need to paint the four walls?

   a) 24 litres

   b) 96 litres

   c) 94 litres

   d) 86 litres

OC MATHS TEST 1

5. Gemma cut a cake in half. She then cut one piece in half again. She then cut one of these pieces in half again, and ate one of these smaller pieces. What fraction represents the amount of cake that Gemma ate?

    a) $^1/_8$

    b) $^1/_2$

    c) $^1/_6$

    d) $^1/_4$

6. Which of the following images does NOT have an axis of symmetry?

a)
b)

c)
d)

7. Which of the following maths equations is incorrect?

    a) $5 \div 5 + 20 = 21$

    b) $5 - 5 \times 20 = 0$

    c) $5 + 5 \times 20 = 105$

    d) $20 \div (5 - 1) = 5$

8. Which of the following sets of metric measurements is ordered from smallest to largest?

    a) 6 g, 25 kg, ½ kg, 400 g

    b) 50 cm, 550 mm, 56 cm, 5 m

    c) 880 g, 8 kg, 9 ½ kg, 900 g

    d) 60 mL, 700 mL, ½ L, 770 mL

OC MATHS TEST 1

9. What is the place value of the underlined digit?

56 7<u>8</u>9 100

a) hundreds

b) thousands

c) ten thousands

d) hundred thousands

10. What number should replace the question mark?

$$90\ 000 + 100 + 1 + 500\ 000 + 10 + \ ? \ = 596\ 111$$

a) 600

b) 6 000

c) 6 100

d) 60 000

11. Aldo owns 2 fully-grown German Shepherds. The total weight of both dogs should be approximately:

a) 5 kg

b) 20 kg

c) 75 kg

d) 200 kg

12. What time is showing on the clock?

a) Eight to two

b) Eight past ten

c) Ten to two

d) Half past ten

OC MATHS TEST 2

1. Ari must tile a bathroom floor which is 40 m² in area. He has finished tiling 25% of the floor. What area of the bathroom floor remains to be tiled?

      a) 30 m²

      b) 25 m²

      c) 35 m²

      d) 10 m²

2. Finola's plane left Sydney at 6 am Monday, and landed in Budapest at 9.30 am Tuesday. How long did the flight take?

      a) 15 hours 30 minutes

      b) 27 hours 30 minutes

      c) 29 hours

      d) 29 hours 30 minutes

3. Which equation is NOT correct?

      a) $8 \times 8 - 50 = 14$

      b) $30 - 9 \times 3 = 3$

      c) $50 + 12 \div 3 = 54$

      d) $70 \div 7 + 3 = 10$

4. If each small square is equal to 10 m² in area, what is the size of the entire shaded area?

      a) 120 m²

      b) 30 m²

      c) 130 m²

      d) 135 m²

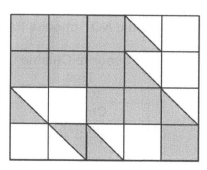

OC MATHS TEST 2

5. Anu has 4 people in her group of friends, including herself. If every person in the group writes a letter to each other person, how many letters are written in total?

a) 4

b) 8

c) 9

d) 12

6. Louie, Chetan and Daniel are playing a game of cards. Daniel has half as many cards as Chetan. Louie has 4 less cards than Daniel. If Louie has 10 cards, how many cards does Chetan have?

a) 14

b) 20

c) 24

d) 28

7. Wanda is saving up to buy an mp3 player which costs $299. If she ears $90 by washing cars, $50 from babysitting, $100 from cleaning the house and $40 from ironing, how much more money does she need?

a) $19

b) $29

c) $39

d) $49

8. How many people did NOT choose Italian as their favourite type of cuisine?

Favourite Cuisine	Number of People
Thai	7
Italian	9
Chinese	10
Indian	8

a) 17

b) 9

c) 25

d) 24

OC MATHS TEST 2

9. In the year 2006, Hadyn turned 58. In what year was Hadyn born?

    a) 1938

    b) 1946

    c) 1948

    d) 1952

10. What is 424 ÷ 4?

    a) 104

    b) 106

    c) 140

    d) 160

11. Mr Dreyfus asked his students to note down the colour of each car as they drove passed their primary school. What was the 2nd most popular colour car?

    a) Red

    b) Blue

    c) Yellow

    d) Green

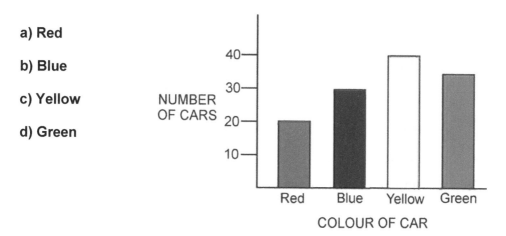

12. Mrs Kensy has 32 students in her class. She tells half of her students to go to the library. She then asks ¼ of the students remaining in the classroom to use the computers. How many students are asked to use the computers?

    a) 4

    b) 8

    c) 12

    d) 16

OC MATHS TEST 3

1. Celia's sister Bethan turned 14 in 2004. Celia is exactly 3 years older than Bethan. In what year was Celia born?

      a) 1987

      b) 1990

      c) 1993

      d) 1994

2. Which of the following sets of numbers are NOT all multiples of 4?

      a) 44, 4, 36, 12

      b) 16, 28, 52, 48

      c) 8, 24, 60, 56

      d) 4, 54, 32, 20

3. What comes next in the following sequence?

$$1, 2, 3, 5, 8, \ldots$$

      a) 10

      b) 11

      c) 12

      d) 13

4. The following can of lemonade is cut in half as shown by the dotted line. Which shape looks most like the face made by the cut?

a)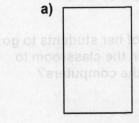

b)

c)

d)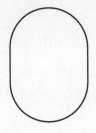

5. Ebony thinks of a number. She multiplies it by 8 and then adds 5. She ends up with 29. What number did Ebony start with?

      a) 2

      b) 3

      c) 4

      d) 5

6. Steven distributes 17 DVDs equally among his 5 grandchildren. How many DVDs does each grandchild receive?

      a) 3 remainder 1

      b) 3 remainder 2

      c) 4 remainder 2

      d) 5 remainder 1

7. Solve the following equation.

$$5 \overline{)520}$$

      a) 14

      b) 140

      c) 150

      d) 104

8. There are 33 students in Mrs Singh's Year 4 class, 28 students in Mr Matthew's Year 4 class, and 29 students in Ms Huppert's Year 4 class. There are twice as many students in Year 4 than in Year 3. How many students are in Year 3?

      a) 45

      b) 60

      c) 90

      d) 180

OC MATHS TEST 3

9. Payal can fit exactly 3 cheese and tomato sandwiches into his lunchbox. Daina's lunchbox is the same size as 3 of Payal's lunchboxes. How many cheese and tomato sandwiches can Daina fit into her lunchbox?

a) 8

b) 7

c) 9

d) 6

10. Which of the following 3-Dimensional shapes is not a prism?

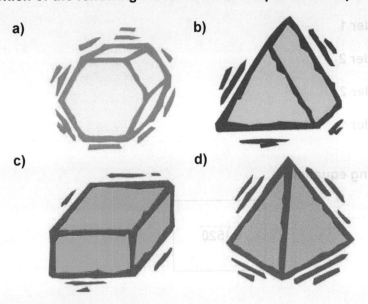

a)

b)

c)

d)

11. What is 5 792 to the nearest ten?

a) 5 700

b) 5 790

c) 5 780

d) 5 785

12. Roberto has $3 in his piggy bank, made up of fifty and twenty cent pieces. He has 9 coins. How many fifty cent pieces does Roberto have?

a) 4

b) 2

c) 8

d) 5

OC MATHS TEST 4

1. Solve the following problem:

> 7 is to week as … is to leap year

    a) 356

    b) 364

    c) 365

    d) 366

2. What is fifty thousand, seven hundred and ninety-two in numerical form?

    a) 57 092

    b) 57 092

    c) 50 792

    d) 5 792

3. Reynato has the following coins in his wallet. If he wants to buy a juice for $4.50, how many more coins does he need?

    a) One 50 cent and two 20 cent coins

    b) Two 50 cent, one 10 cent and one 5 cent coin

    c) One 50 cent, one 10 cent and one 5 cent coin

    d) One dollar, one 10 cent and three 5 cent coins

4. Which of the following sets of numbers are NOT all multiples of 3?

    a) 18, 15, 30, 43

    b) 39, 3, 6, 9

    c) 24, 21, 42, 36

    d) 45, 9, 27, 33

OC MATHS TEST 4

Questions 5 to 7 relate to the following information:

SCRUMPTIOUS STRAWBERRY SMOOTHIES

Ingredients:

- 350 g strawberries
- 750 mL milk
- 2 scoops vanilla ice cream
- 2 tbsp honey

Method:

Peel and chop mangoes into cubes. Place all ingredients in a blender. Blend at high speed for 3 minutes. Pour into 2 long glasses and serve immediately.
Serves 2.

Magda decides to make Succulent Strawberry Smoothies for 3 friends and herself, using the recipe above.

5. What amount of strawberries and ice cream will Magda need to serve everyone?

   a) 350 g strawberries and 1500 mL milk

   b) 750 g strawberries and 750 mL milk

   c) 700 g strawberries and 1500 mL milk

   d) 1400 g strawberries and 3000 mL milk

6. If 8 strawberries weigh 200g, approximately how many strawberries are needed to make the recipe for Magda and her friends?

   a) 8

   b) 16

   c) 24

   d) 28

OC MATHS TEST 4

7. If one 350 g punnet of strawberries costs $2.75 and milk costs $0.50 for every 250 mL, how much will the strawberries and milk cost to serve all four people?

   a) $8.50

   b) $6.75

   c) $7

   d) $17

8. Solve the following equation.

$$(3 \times 8) - [] = 20$$

   a) 3

   b) 4

   c) 6

   d) 8

9. How many litres are in 35 000 mL?

   a) 35 000 000 L

   b) 35 000 L

   c) 350 L

   d) 35 L

10. Marc starts at the petrol station. He drives 20 km east. He then drives 50 km south. He then drives 20 km west and arrives at his house. In what direction is Marc's home from the petrol station?

   a) south

   b) south east

   c) east

   d) south west

OC MATHS TEST 5

1. What is the first prime number that comes after 19?

    a) 21

    b) 23

    c) 27

    d) 29

2. Which rectangle has $\frac{1}{3}$ of its area shaded in?

a)

b)

c)

d)

3. Louis started with a number and multiplied it by two. He then divided the answer by four and was left with 18. What number did Louis start with?

    a) 72

    b) 28

    c) 36

    d) 62

4. There are 100 students in Year Four. 48% of the students are boys. What percentage of students are girls?

    a) 2%

    b) 42%

    c) 48%

    d) 52%

OC MATHS TEST 5

5. Bridget takes 150 seconds to brush her teeth in the morning. How many minutes is this?

    a) 1 $\frac{1}{2}$ minutes

    b) 2 $\frac{1}{2}$ minutes

    c) 3 minutes

    d) 3 $\frac{1}{2}$ minutes

6. Mischa is 4 years older than Prianka. Prianka is half the age of Nicole. If Nicole is 30, how old is Mischa?

    a) 19

    b) 11

    c) 34

    d) 23

7. Leigh goes to the fruit and vegetable shop. Bananas are selling at 6 for $3.00, pears are selling for 5 for $2.00 and apples are selling at 55 cents each. Which fruit costs the most per item?

    a) Bananas

    b) Pears

    c) Apples

    d) They all cost the same

8. Which of the following numbers are in order from largest to smallest?

    a) 2, 1.9, 1.5, 1.7

    b) 2, 1.9, 1.7, 1.5

    c) 1.5, 1.7, 1.9. 2

    d) 1.9, 1.7, 1.5, 2

OC MATHS TEST 5

9. Which student has read less than 30 books?

a) Cary

b) Jacinta

c) Lawrence

d) Van

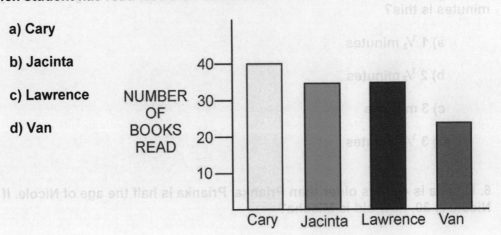

10. The product of a number and 10 is 170. What is this number?

a) 11

b) 7

c) 17

d) 71

11. Solve the following equation.

$$[\ ] - 15 + (5 \times 10) = 60$$

a) 25

b) 27

c) 30

d) 35

12. Avindran went to bed at 8:30 pm and awoke the next morning at 6:00 am. How many hours of sleep did Avindran receive?

a) 8 ½

b) 9 ½

c) 10 ½

d) 12 ½

OC MATHS TEST 6

Questions 1 and 2 relate to the following information.

Cecile surveyed a group of Year 4 students about their favourite movie genre and drew up the following table

FAVOURITE GENRE	NUMBER OF STUDENTS
Comedy	15
Action	4
Sci-fi	9
Drama	11

1. How many students' favourite genre was NOT comedy?

   a) 15

   b) 20

   c) 24

   d) 28

2. How many students' favourite genre was either comedy or sci-fi?

   a) 15

   b) 24

   c) 27

   d) 30

3. The numbers in the following pyramid form a pattern. What number should replace the question mark?

   a) 1

   b) 2

   c) 3

   d) 4

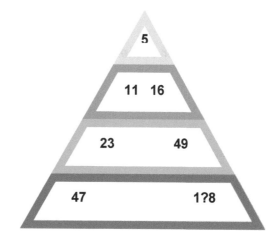

OC MATHS TEST 6

4. How many years are there in 12 centuries and 6 decades?

    a) 126 060 years

    b) 126 years

    c) 260 years

    d) 1 260 years

Questions 5 and 6 relate to the following information.

Richard wants to build a fence to enclose the sheep on his farm. He draws the following diagram to show the area of the fence.

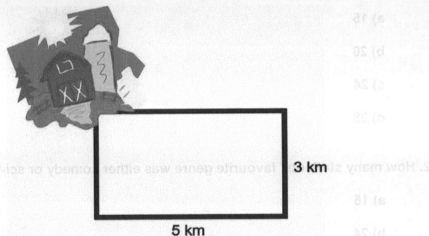

3 km

5 km

5. Approximately what area will the fence enclose?

    a) 8 km²

    b) 15 km²

    c) 16 km²

    d) 30 km²

6. What is the perimeter of the fence?

    a) 15 km

    b) 16 km

    c) 18 km

    d) 20 km

OC MATHS TEST 6

7. Which number is missing from the following equation?

$$\begin{array}{r} 73\ - \\ \underline{3?} \\ \underline{42} \end{array}$$

    a) 1

    b) 2

    c) 3

    d) 4

8. Zaahir took a train from Central Station to Brisbane Station. The journey took 11 hours and 30 minutes. If the train arrived at Brisbane Station at 5:00 am, at what time did the train depart from Central Station?

    a) 5:30 pm

    b) 6:30 pm

    c) 5:30 am

    d) 6:30 am

9. Which of the following sets of numbers are NOT all multiples of 8?

    a) 48, 8, 32, 104

    b) 16, 24, 88, 96

    c) 40, 112, 80, 56

    d) 36, 64, 32, 88

10. Kathryn picked 10 apples off a tree. She then ate 3. Which calculation shows how many apples are left over?

    a) $10 \div 3 = 3\,\tfrac{1}{3}$

    b) $3 - 10 = -7$

    c) $10 - 3 = 7$

    d) $3 + 10 = 13$

OC MATHS TEST 7

1. Which of the following can form the net of a cube?

a)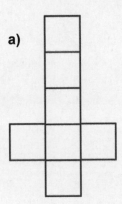

b)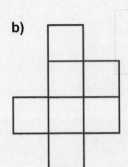

c)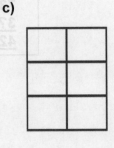

d)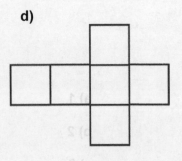

2. The length of a square is twice as long as 5cm. What is the perimeter of the square?

a) 20 cm

b) 25 cm

c) 40 cm

d) 100 cm

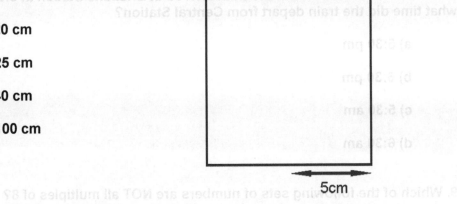

5cm

3. Which of the following numbers are in order from smallest to largest?

a) 11.1, 9.7, 9.9, 11.0

b) 11.0, 9.9, 11.1, 9.7

c) 9.7, 9.9. 11.1, 11.0

d) 9.7, 9.9, 11.0, 11.1

4. In his last maths test, Pablo scored 75%. If there were a total of 40 marks in the test, what was Pablo's score?

a) 25

b) 30

c) 35

d) 75

OC MATHS TEST 7

5. What time is showing on this watch?

    a) 7:15

    b) 7:45

    c) 8:15

    d) 8:45

6. The product of a number and 7 is 42. What is this number?

    a) 6

    b) 7

    c) 8

    d) 9

7. How many eggs in 3 dozen?

    a) 31

    b) 33

    c) 34

    d) 36

8. Which number is missing from the following equation?

$$\begin{array}{r} 64\ - \\ \underline{2?} \\ \underline{39} \end{array}$$

    a) 3

    b) 5

    c) 7

    d) 9

OC MATHS TEST 7

9.

$$22 \div 3 =$$

a) 6 remainder 1

b) 6 remainder 2

c) 7 remainder 1

d) 7 remainder 211

10. The following top hat is cut in half as shown by the dotted line. Which shape looks most like the face made by the cut?

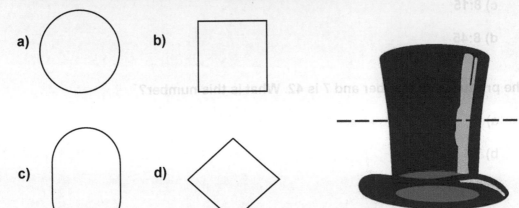

a)

b)

c)

d)

11. George's grandmother cut a cherry pie into 8 even pieces. George then ate 2 pieces of pie. Which fraction best represents the amount of pie that George ate?

a) $\frac{1}{2}$

b) $\frac{1}{4}$

c) $\frac{1}{8}$

d) $\frac{3}{4}$

12. Cassandra starts with a number, which she divides by 3. She then adds 2. She is left with the number 5. What number did Cassandra start with?

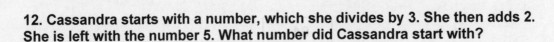

a) 18

b) 15

c) 12

d) 9

OC MATHS TEST 8

1. Frederic has to buy a case for his reading glasses below. Approximately how large should the base area of the case be? (glasses are drawn to scale)

a) 5 cm by 6 cm

b) 5 cm by 13 cm

c) 8 cm by 9 cm

d) 2 cm by 10 cm

2. Which number is missing from the following equation?

$$\begin{array}{r} 61\ + \\ 3? \\ \hline 99 \end{array}$$

a) 2

b) 4

c) 6

d) 8

3. Anna has the following notes in her wallet. How much money is in Anna's wallet?

a) $55.20

b) $70.15

c) $75.00

d) $85.00

OC MATHS TEST 8

4. Evan rolls a dice. What is the chance that he rolls an even number?

    a) ¼

    b) ½

    c) ⅓

    d) ⅛

5. Riley went on a trip from Sydney to Canberra. The trip lasted a total of 36 hours. If he returned to Sydney at 4:00 pm on Monday, at what time did he depart from Sydney?

    a) 4:00 pm Saturday

    b) 8:00 pm Saturday

    c) 4:00 am Sunday

    d) 4:00 pm Sunday

6. What comes next in the following sequence?

$$2, 4, 8, 16, \ldots$$

    a) 18

    b) 20

    c) 32

    d) 36

7. How many seconds in 4 and a half minutes?

    a) 210

    b) 270

    c) 430

    d) 450

OC MATHS TEST 8

Questions 8 and 9 relate to the following information and table.

Mr O'Neil had 28 students in his class. He divided his class into those who wear glasses all the time, those who wear glasses only for reading and those who do not wear glasses. Mr O'Neil then drew up the following table.

CATEGORY	NUMBER OF STUDENTS
Always wear glasses	6
Wear glasses for reading	7
Do not wear glasses	15

8. How many students either always wear glasses or wear glasses for reading?

   a) 6

   b) 7

   c) 13

   d) 15

9. How many more students do not wear glasses compared to those students that always wear glasses?

   a) 9

   b) 11

   c) 15

   d) 7

10. The difference in distance between Lucy and Harry's house is 20 kilometres. If Lucy is driving at 40 km/h, how many minutes will it take Lucy to drive to Harry's house?

   a) 30 minutes

   b) 50 minutes

   c) 60 minutes

   d) 120 minutes

OC MATHS TEST 9

1. If an upright apple is rotated at an angle of 90° in a clockwise direction, what would it look like?

a)

b)

c)

d)

2. The sum of a number and 53 is 65. What is this number?

a) 8

b) 9

c) 11

d) 12

3. Solve the following equation.

$$24 \div 3 - 8 = ?$$

a) 0

b) 1

c) 1 ½

d) 4

4. Amelie and her brother Frederic are 18 months apart in age. Amelie is the eldest child. If Amelie was born on 5 May 1996, when was Frederic born?

a) 5 March 1995

b) 5 November 1996

c) 5 December 1996

d) 5 November 1997

OC MATHS TEST 9

5. XV + III – IV =

    a) CX

    b) XII

    c) XIV

    d) IV

6. If 3 ! 4 # 5 = 7, and 13 # 9 ! 1 = 4, what do the # and the ! represent?

    a) ! represents ÷ and # represents –

    b) ! represents ÷ and # represents +

    c) ! represents × and # represents ÷

    d) ! represents × and # represents –

7. How many triangles are in this shape?

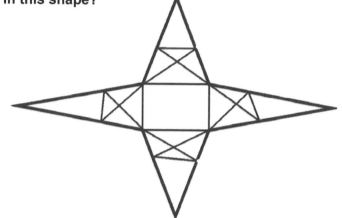

    a) 24

    b) 32

    c) 48

    d) 96

8. Darna buys a $2.10 notepad, a $1.25 pen and two 40 cent lollipops. She pays with a $5 note. How much change should Dana receive?

    a) $4.15

    b) $1.00

    c) 95 cents

    d) 85 cents

OC MATHS TEST 9

9.

$$3 \times \tfrac{1}{4} + 4 \times \tfrac{1}{2} + \tfrac{1}{4} = ?$$

a) 2 ½

b) 2 ¾

c) 3

d) 3 ¼

10. In Mr Gutridge's class there are 9 more boys than girls. How many students are in Mr Gutridge's class if there are 12 girls?

a) 30 students

b) 33 students

c) 21 students

d) 19 students

11. Which number should replace the question mark to complete the pattern?

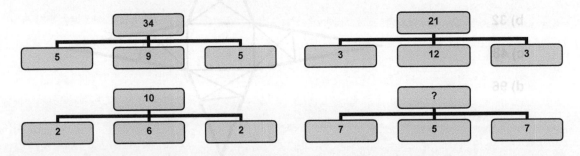

a) 19

b) 33

c) 42

d) 54

12. How many integers between 1 and 100 are multiples of 3?

a) 99

b) 36

c) 33

d) 30

OC MATHS TEST 10

1. Campbell's birthday is 51 days before Mariska's. If Campbell's birthday is 21 September, what date is Mariska's birthday?

    a) 10 November

    b) 11 November

    c) 10 October

    d) 1 August

Questions 2 to 5 relate to the following graph.

Mrs Macarthur interviewed her Year 4 class and asked each student how many siblings they had. She then graphed the results.

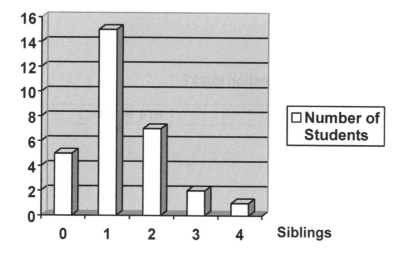

2. How many students had exactly 2 siblings?

    a) 5

    b) 13

    c) 6

    d) 7

3. How many students had less than 3 siblings?

    a) 27

    b) 26

    c) 20

    d) 2

4. How many students had an odd number of siblings?

    a) 4

    b) 11

    c) 15

    d) 17

5. What was the least popular number of siblings?

    a) 0

    b) 1

    c) 3

    d) 4

6. What number should replace the question mark?

654 ▶ 15 ▶ 6	876 ▶ ? ▶ 3

    a) 19

    b) 21

    c) 23

    d) 25

7. Lateefa rolls a dice. What is the chance that she rolls an even number or a 1?

    a) $\frac{1}{6}$

    b) $\frac{4}{6}$

    c) $\frac{2}{6}$

    d) $\frac{3}{6}$

OC MATHS TEST 10

8. Hal picks out a number between 1 and 50. The sum of the two digits is 9. The two digits multiply to give 14. What is this number?

    a) 51

    b) 34

    c) 43

    d) 27

9. A frame is constructed with timber 1 cm in width (drawn below). What is the perimeter of the outside edge of the frame?

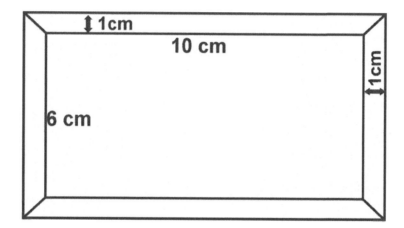

    a) 96 cm

    b) 40 cm

    b) 36 cm

    d) 20 cm

10. What comes next in the following sequence?

$$3, 5, 8, 13, \ldots$$

    a) 13

    b) 16

    c) 18

    d) 21

OC MATHS TEST 11

1. Jamison runs the 800 metres race in 5 minutes. If he runs at the same pace, how long does it take Jamison to run 1 200 metres?

    a) 7 ½ minutes

    b) 8 minutes

    c) 7 minutes

    d) 9 ½ minutes

2. What comes next in the following sequence?

$$2, 6, 14, 30, \ldots$$

    a) 62

    b) 34

    c) 68

    d) 48

3. What is ¼ × 6 × 2?

    a) 1

    b) 3

    c) 6

    d) 8

4. Which of the following numbers is NOT a factor of 96?

    a) 4

    b) 12

    c) 16

    d) 18

5. Damien buys 5 pot plants. He needs to fill each pot with 2 ½ kilograms of soil. If Damien has 15 kilograms of soil, how much soil will be left over after he fills all 5 pots?

      a) 12 kilograms

      b) 6 ½ kilograms

      c) 3 ½ kilograms

      d) 2 ½ kilograms

Questions 6 to 8 relate to the following information.

Erica leaves school at 3:00 pm and cycles 2.5 km east to go to the gym. She arrives at the gym at 3:15 pm. After 45 minutes at the gym, Erica then cycles back to her school and a further 10 km to get to the local café. It takes Erica half an hour to cycle from the gym to the café. She leaves the café 20 minutes later.

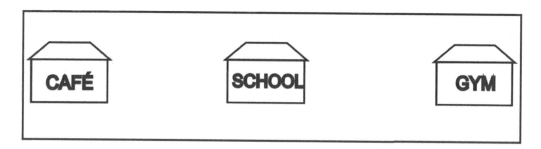

6. How many kilometres does Erica cycle altogether?

      a) 5 km

      b) 10 km

      c) 15 km

      d) 20 km

7. At what time does Erica leave the café?

      a) 4:30 pm

      b) 4:50 pm

      c) 5:30 pm

      d) 5:50 pm

OC MATHS TEST 11

8. In what direction is the school from the café?

    a) East

    b) West

    c) North

    d) South

9. What is five multiplied by three plus five squared?

    a) 40

    b) 35

    c) 25

    d) 23

10. What number's triple exceeds its half by exactly 30?

    a) 6

    b) 8

    c) 10

    d) 12

11. Complete the following pattern.

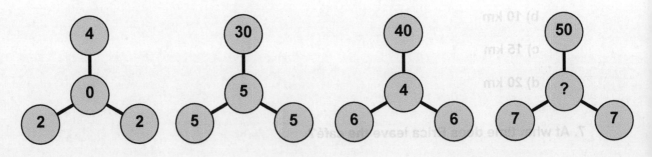

    a) 1

    b) 3

    c) 6

    d) 7

OC MATHS TEST 12

1. A rectangle's length is twice the size of its breadth. If the length of the rectangle is 12 cm, what is the area of the rectangle?

     a) 36 cm²

     b) 66 cm²

     c) 72 cm²

     d) 240 cm²

2. Which of the following letters has the highest number of axes of symmetry?

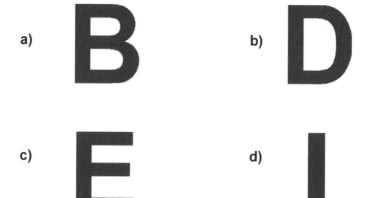

a) B   b) D

c) E   d) I

3. A tap is dripping water into a bucket at the rate of 25 drops per minute. 100 drops is equal to 80 mL of water. How many mL of water are in the tank after 12 minutes?

     a) 240 mL

     b) 300 mL

     c) 960 mL

     d) 1200 mL

4. Petra owns a slow alarm clock, which loses 3 minutes every hour. When she checks her clock the time is 9:00 am. Petra checks the clock 6 hours later. What time does the slow alarm clock display?

     a) 13:45

     b) 14:42

     c) 14:46

     d) 15:16

OC MATHS TEST 12

Questions 5 and 6 relate to the following information.

Alix's father has a total of 45 pearls to give out to his daughters. He gives twice as many pearls to Susannah as he does to Alix. Alix receives one quarter of the amount of pearls that Marianne receives. Lotte receives half as many pearls as Marianne.

5. Which 2 daughters receive the same number of pearls?

    a) Alix and Susannah

    b) Alix and Lotte

    c) Susannah and Lotte

    d) Marianne and Susannah

6. How many pearls does Marianne receive from her father?

    a) 5

    b) 10

    c) 20

    d) 25

7. Russel is facing South East. He then turns around at an angle of 180°. In what direction is Russel now facing?

    a) North West

    b) South East

    c) West

    d) South West

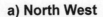

8. Complete the following sequence:

21, 7, 42, 14, …

    a) 28

    b) 7

    c) 68

    d) 84

OC MATHS TEST 12

9. What is the total perimeter of this shape?

   a) 36 cm

   b) 56 cm

   c) 58 cm

   d) 78 cm

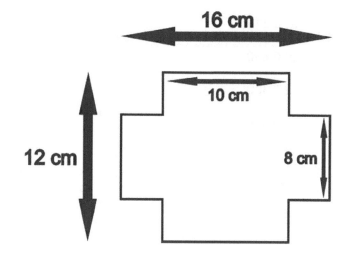

10. How many minutes are in 4 ½ hours?

   a) 450

   b) 310

   c) 430

   d) 270

11. Which number should replace the question mark in the following equation?

$$3 + (?) - 5 \times 2 = 5$$

   a) 18

   b) 7

   c) 12

   d) 5

12. On Monday, Bianca makes an appointment to see the doctor in 16 days. On what day will Bianca go to see the doctor?

   a) Monday

   b) Tuesday

   c) Wednesday

   d) Thursday

OC MATHS TEST 13

1. What is 6 377 to the nearest hundred?

    a) 6 370

    b) 6 400

    c) 6 300

    d) 6 380

2. Madeleine's house is 28km directly south of the library, and 15km directly north of the post office. How far away is the post office from the library?

    a) 13 km

    b) 23 km

    c) 33 km

    d) 43 km

3. How many 250 mL poppers are needed to fill a 5 L container of juice?

    a) 4

    b) 10

    c) 15

    d) 20

4. Which of the following numbers is NOT a factor of 154?

    a) 7

    b) 11

    c) 19

    d) 22

OC MATHS TEST 13

Questions 5 and 6 relate to the following diagram.

5. What is the perimeter of Charlotte's school playground drawn below?
(diagram not to scale)

a) 525 m

b) 425 m

c) 485 m

d) 585 m

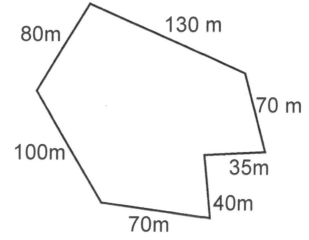

6. The perimeter of Charlotte's playground is 5 times larger than Gordon's playground. What is the perimeter of Gordon's playground?

a) 55 m

b) 105 m

c) 155 m

d) 225 m

7. What fraction of the rectangle is shaded in?

a) $\frac{1}{3}$

b) $\frac{1}{4}$

c) $\frac{1}{2}$

d) $\frac{1}{8}$

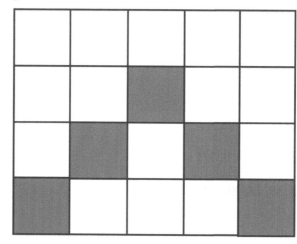

8. Carl thinks of three different odd numbers. The sum of the three numbers is 41. If one of the numbers is 9, which of the following pairs of numbers could the other two be?

a) 20 and 12

b) 13 and 15

c) 17 and 13

d) 19 and 13

9. Max was at the train station. He walked 10 km north. He then walked 10 km west and arrived at his house. In what direction is the train station from Max's house?

a) south east

b) north east

c) south west

d) north west

10. In how many different ways can the letters ABC be arranged?

a) 9

b) 6

c) 12

d) 3

11. Which of the following sets of roman numerals is in ascending order (from lowest to highest)?

a) VI, XII, IX, XV

b) IX, XII, VI, XV

c) VI, IX, XV, XII

d) VI, IX, XII, XV

OC MATHS TEST 14

1. Reece sticks together a triangular pyramid and a triangular prism to make the 3D shape below.

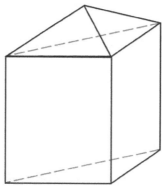

How many vertices does the shape have?

      a) 6

      b) 7

      c) 8

      d) 9

2. How would one million, seventeen-thousand, seven hundred and eighty-four be written in numerical form?

      a) 1 177 840

      b) 117 784

      c) 1 017 784

      d) 170 784

3. Cameron flies from Sydney where the temperature is 27°C, to Seoul where the temperature is − 4°C. How much cooler is it in Seoul in comparison to Sydney?

      a) 31°C

      b) 27°C

      c) 24°C

      d) 23°C

OC MATHS TEST 14

4. Jade added 52 to 49 and 24. She then rounded her answer to the nearest ten. What should Jade's answer be?

      a) 100

      b) 120

      c) 130

      d) 140

5. What number should replace the question mark in the following equation?

$$600 \div ? = 8$$

      a) 70

      b) 72

      c) 75

      d) 120

6. What is the approximate length of the watch?

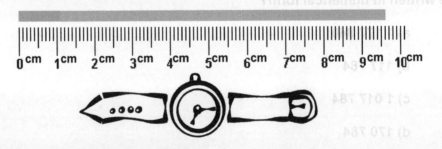

      a) 5 centimetres and 9 millimetres

      b) 6 centimetres and 2 millimetres

      c) 6 centimetres and 9 millimetres

      d) 7 centimetres and 3 millimetres

7. Nasser cycles 30 kilometres in 120 minutes. How many minutes does it take Nasser to cycle 10 kilometres?

      a) 40 minutes

      b) 30 minutes

      c) 45 minutes

      d) 10 minutes

8. The average score in a Year 4 general knowledge test was 40 out of 50. What would this score be if it was converted to a percentage?

    a) 40%

    b) 50%

    c) 75%

    d) 80%

9. There are 5 children in Millie's family. Millie is shorter than Mark. Agatha is taller than Tim. Floyd is taller than Mark. Millie is taller than Agatha. Put the children in height order from tallest to shortest.

    a) Mark Tim Millie Floyd Agatha

    b) Floyd Mark Millie Agatha Tim

    c) Floyd Mark Agatha Tim Millie

    d) Floyd Mark Millie Tim Agatha

10. Which of the following can form a triangular prism:

a) 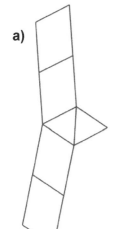 b) 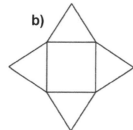 c) 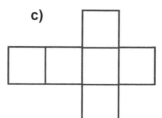 d)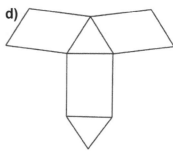

11. What is another way to write 7^2?

    a) 7 × 2

    b) 7 × 7

    c) 2^2× 2^2

    d) 7 × 7 × 7 × 7 × 7 × 7 × 7

OC MATHS TEST 15

1. What comes next in the following sequence?

$$0, 1, 2, 6, 16, 44, \ldots$$

      a) 60

      b) 64

      c) 84

      d) 120

2. I have 2 circular faces and 2 circular edges. I do not have a vertex. What am I?

      a) a triangular prism

      b) a sphere

      c) a cube

      d) a cylinder

Questions 3 and 4 relate to the following information:

Tyron interviewed 100 ten year olds on what was their favourite meal. 29 children preferred pizza, 37 preferred hamburgers, 15 preferred sushi and the remaining children preferred fish and chips.

3. What percentage of children decided fish and chips was their favourite meal?

      a) 21%

      b) 19%

      c) 29%

      d) 11%

4. What percentage of children did NOT choose pizza as their favourite meal?

      a) 71%

      b) 69%

      c) 81%

      d) 29%

OC MATHS TEST 15

5. What is 12 000 000 + 400 000 + 500 + 70 + 9

   a) 124 579

   b) 12 040 579

   c) 12 450 709

   d) 12 400 579

Questions 6 and 7 relate to the following information.

The following magic square uses nine different numbers in between 0 and 10.
All the rows add up to 15.

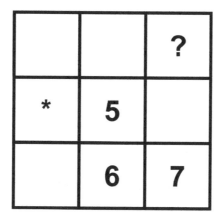

6. What number should replace the question mark?

   a) 8

   b) 4

   c) 9

   d) 3

7. What number should replace the star?

   a) 10

   b) 9

   c) 8

   d) 7

OC MATHS TEST 15

8. What number should come next in the following series?

> 1523, 2634, 3745, ...

a) 2364

b) 4856

c) 5473

d) 2856

9. Zachary needs to purchase 10 tangelos. He sees the following signs at the fruit market:

Tangelos sold separately = $3.50 each!

Packet of 2 tangelos for $5.00!

Box of 5 tangelos = $10.50!

How can Zachary purchase 10 tangelos for the least amount of money?

a) Buy 10 tangelos separately

b) Buy one box of 5 tangelos, and purchase the rest separately.

c) Buy 5 packets of 2 tangelos

d) Buy 2 boxes of 5 tangelos

10. A pair of musical notes is rotated at an angle of 180°.
What does the pair of musical notes look like after the rotation?

a)

b)

c)

d)

OC MATHS TEST 16

1. Molly's car consumes 18 litres of petrol every 100 kilometres. If Molly travels 250 kilometres, how much petrol will her car consume?

    a) 14 litres

    b) 36 litres

    c) 45 litres

    d) 450 litres

Questions 2 to 4 relate to the following information and table.

Chase grew an orange tree, an apple tree and a pear tree in his backyard. After 1 year Chase counted how many fruit were on each tree. He then drew up the following table.

Type of Tree	Number of Fruit
Orange	⊬⊬ ⊬⊬ ⊬⊬
Apple	⊬⊬ ⊬⊬ ⊬⊬ ///
Pear	⊬⊬ ⊬⊬ //

2. How many oranges are growing on Chase's orange tree?

    a) 12

    b) 15

    c) 17

    d) 18

3. How many pieces of fruit are there altogether?

    a) 50

    b) 47

    c) 37

    d) 45

OC MATHS TEST 16

4. How many more apples than pears are there?

    a) 1

    b) 3

    c) 4

    d) 6

5. What is 25% of $44?

    a) $2.50

    b) $10

    c) $11

    d) $25

6. Nikolas bought 3 and a half kilograms of bananas at $5.50 per kilo. How much money did the bananas cost Nikolas?

    a) $19.25

    b) $15.50

    c) $19.95

    d) $17.75

7. How many years in 3 centuries and 4 decades?

    a) 70 years

    b) 700 years

    c) 340 years

    d) 34 years

OC MATHS TEST 16

8. Sophia sends her friend a postcard from Paris (pictured below). She attaches a stamp to the postcard. The area of the postcard is 9 times larger than the area of the stamp. What is the area of the stamp?

a) 7 cm²

b) 32 cm²

c) 9 cm²

d) 63 cm²

7 cm

9 cm

9. The following pairs of numbers follow the same pattern. What number should replace the question mark?

33 ~ 12

27 ~ 10

54 ~ 19

48 ~ ?

a) 12

b) 15

c) 17

d) 18

10. A bag containing 9 packets of chips weighs 700 grams. What is the approximate weight of 1 packet of chips?

a) 74 grams

b) 129 grams

c) 78 grams

d) 81 grams

OC MATHS EXTENSION

1. Complete the following sequence:

64, 49, 36, ...

a) 22

b) 18

c) 29

d) 25

2. Jonathan has 3 tables in his dining room. Each table has 4 legs. He also has a number of chairs. Each chair has 4 legs. There are a total of 32 legs in Jonathan's dining room. Helen has twice as many chairs as Jonathan in her dining room. How many chairs are in Helen's dining room?

a) 5

b) 6

c) 8

d) 10

3. What number can replace both the question marks in the following equation?

?4 –
2?
38

a) 5

b) 6

c) 7

d) 8

4. Marie thinks of four different numbers. The numbers have a product of 84 and a sum of 15. What could the four numbers be?

a) 8 4 2 1

b) 9 8 4 3

c) 6 1 3 7

d) 4 7 1 3

OC MATHS EXTENSION

5. Emile receives a $60 gift voucher. He purchases 2 books at $13.95 each and a DVD for $18. He then buys a notepad for ¼ the price of the DVD. How much money does Emile have left over to spend with his gift voucher?

      a) $9.20

      b) $9.60

      c) $5.20

      d) $12.40

6. Aimee purchases the following two cartons of milk from the supermarket.

Aimee wants to pour 8 glasses of milk. What volume of milk will each glass hold?

      a) ¼ L

      b) 200 mL

      c) 400 mL

      d) ½ L

7. Complete the following equation:

$$12 \div \tfrac{1}{4} = ?$$

      a) 48

      b) 3

      c) ½

      d) ¼

OC MATHS EXTENSION

8. Aiden's mother is turning 30 in 2008. If Aiden is 21 years younger than his mother, in what year was Aiden born?

    a) 1978

    b) 1988

    c) 1999

    d) 2000

9. Solve the following problem:

ME + YOU = BEAFEF

UP + OUT = AEDBCF

IN + ON = ?

    a) CFECBF

    b) CFECC

    c) FEAB

    d) BDBH

Questions 10 and 11 relate to the following information.

10. Blake empties one 250 mL cup of water into an empty 20 litre bucket every 5 seconds. How long will it take Blake to fill the bucket with water?

    a) 4 minutes

    b) 5 minutes

    c) 6 minutes 35 seconds

    d) 6 minutes 40 seconds.

11. How long will it take Blake to fill the bucket if it already has 3 litres of water in it?

    a) 5 minutes 35 seconds

    b) 3 minutes 50 seconds

    c) 5 minutes 40 seconds

    d) 3 minutes 40 seconds

OC MATHS EXTENSION

12. Brent has 3 spiders, 2 ants and 1 millipede in his jar of creepy-crawlies (the millipede has exactly 130 pairs of legs). How many legs are there in Brent's jar?

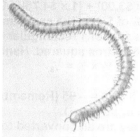

    a) 160

    b) 306

    c) 296

    d) 260

13. Kunal has 7 Labradors and 3 Beagles. Every night, each Labrador is fed 700 grams of canned meat and each Beagle is fed 550 grams of canned meat. What is the minimum amount of canned meat that Kunal will need to feed all the dogs for 2 nights?

    a) 1 350 grams

    b) 13 750 grams

    c) 7 450 grams

    d) 13 100 grams

14. How many of the smaller cubes pictured are able to fit into the larger plastic container?

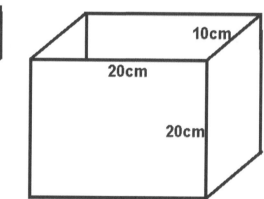

    a) 4

    b) 16

    c) 24

    d) 42

15. Herbert's novel had six chapters in it. The 1st three chapters had the same number of pages. The next two chapters each had 1 ½ times as many pages as the 3rd chapter. The last chapter had ½ as many pages as the 5th chapter. If the 6 chapters were a total of 135 pages, how long was the 3rd chapter?

    a) 18 pages

    b) 20 pages

    c) 10 pages

    d) 15 pages

ANSWERS AND EXPLANATIONS

OC MATHS TEST 1

1. d.
2. d. (2 × $3.00) + (1 × $4.75) + $3.75 = $14.50.
3. d. 50% of $48 is the same as ½ of $48 or $48 ÷ 2 = $24.
4. b. The area of 1 rectangular wall is 4 × 6 = 24 metres squared. As there are 4 walls, 4 × 24 = 96 metres squared. Hence Seong needs 96 litres of paint.
5. a. 1 × ½ × ½ × ½ = $^1/_8$.
6. d.
7. b. 5 – 5 × 20 = – 95 (Remember your order of operations: divide or multiply before you add or subtract).
8. b. If they are all converted to centimetres, then 50 cm, 550 mm, 56 cm, 5 m = 50 cm, 55 cm, 56 cm and 500 cm.
9. c.
10. b. 500 000 + 90 000 + 6 000 + 100 + 10 + 1 = 596 111.
11. c.
12. b.

OC MATHS TEST 2

1. a. 25% is the same as ¼. As ¼ of 40 m² = 10 m², this means that 30 m² of tiling remains to be completed.
2. b. 6 am Monday + 24 hours (1 day) = 6 am Tuesday. Add another 3 hours and 30 minutes to reach 9.30 am. 24 hours + 3 hours and 30 minutes = 27 hours and 30 minutes.
3. d. 70 ÷ 7 + 3 = 13.
4. a. There are 9 full squares shaded in and 6 half squares shaded in, which all together makes 12 full squares. 12 × 10m² = 120 m².
5. d. Each person must write a letter to the 3 other members of the group. As there are 4 members in the group, 3 + 3 + 3 + 3 = 12.
6. d. If Louie has 10 cards, then Daniel has 14 cards (4 more than Louie) and Chetan has 28 Cards (twice as many as Daniel).
7. a. $90 + $50 + $100 + $40 = $280. $299 – $280 = $19.
8. c. 7 + 10 + 8 = 25.
9. c.
10. b. $4\overline{)424}$ with 106 above.
11. d.
12. a. ½ × 32 = 16. ¼ × 16 = 4.

OC MATHS TEST 3

1. a. If Bethan turned 14 in 2004, then Bethan was born in 1990. As Celia is 3 years older than Bethan, Celia must be born in 1987.
2. d. 54 is not a multiple of 4.
3. d. Each number is the sum of the two numbers that come before it i.e. 1 + 2 = 3, 2 + 3 = 5, 3 + 5 = 8, 8 + 5 = 13.
4. a.
5. b. Working backwards, 29 – 5 = 24 and 24 ÷ 8 = 3.
6. b. 17 ÷ 5 = 3 remainder 2.
7. d.
8. a. 33 + 28 + 29 = 90. ½ × 90 = 45.
9. c. 3 × 3 = 9.
10. d. It is a pyramid, not a prism.
11. b.
12. a. Roberto must have 4 fifty cent pieces and 5 twenty cent pieces as 4 × 50 + 5 × 20 = 300.

ANSWERS AND EXPLANATIONS

OC MATHS TEST 4

1. d. There are 7 days in a week, and there are 366 days in a leap year.
2. c.
3. c. Reynato has $3.85, so he needs $0.65 extra to reach $4.50 i.e. one 50 cent, one 10 cent and one 5 cent coin.
4. a. 43 is not a multiple of 3.
5. c. Magda has to serve 4 people, but the recipe only serves 2, so Magda would have to double the quantities which are provided in the recipe.
6. d. If 8 strawberries weigh 200 g, then 4 strawberries weigh 100 g. Magda needs 700 g of strawberries, which is 7 lots of 100 g. 7 × 4 strawberries = 28 strawberries.
7. a. Magda needs 2 punnets of strawberries so 2 × $2.75 = $5.50. She also requires 1500 mL of milk and 1500 ml ÷ 250 mL = 6, so 6 × $0.50 = $3.00. $5.50 + $3.00 = $8.50.
8. b.
9. d. There are 1000 mL in one litre. 35 000 ÷ 1000 = 35.
10. a.

OC MATHS TEST 5

1. b. A prime number is a number that has only two factors; itself and 1.
2. b. The larger rectangle is broken up into 6 equal smaller rectangles, and 2 of the 6 smaller rectangles are shaded in. $\frac{2}{6} = \frac{1}{3}$
3. c. Working backwards, 18 × 4 = 72. 72 ÷ 2 = 36.
4. d. 100% − 48% = 52%.
5. b. There are 60 seconds in a minute. 150 ÷ 60 = 2 minutes and 30 seconds.
6. a. If Nicole is 30 years old, Prianka is ½ of 30, so Prianka is 15 years old. As Mischa is 4 years older than Prianka, 15 + 4 = 19. So Mischa is 19 years old.
7. c. $3.00 ÷ 6 = $0.50 so bananas are 50 cents each. $2.00 ÷ 5 = $0.40 so pears are 40 cents each.
8. b.
9. d.
10. c. 170 ÷ 10 = 17 (or 10 × 17 = 170).
11. a.
12. b.

OC MATHS TEST 6

1. c. If the students' favourite genre was not comedy, it was either action, sci-fi or drama. 4 + 9 + 11 = 24.
2. b. 15 + 9 = 24.
3. d. The numbers on the left are doubled, then one is added to the result. The numbers on the right are tripled, and then one is added to the result. 49 × 3 + 1 = 148.
4. d. There are 100 years in a century and 10 years in a decade. 12 × 100 + 6 × 10 = 1 260 years.
5. b. The area of a rectangle is length × width. 5 km × 3 km = 15 km².
6. b. 5 + 5 + 3 + 3 = 16 km.
7. a.
8. a. 5:30 pm + 6 ½ hours = 12 am. 5 hours later it is 5:00 am. 6 ½ + 5 = 11 ½ hours or 11 hours and 30 minutes.
9. d. 36 is not a multiple of 8.
10. c.

ANSWERS AND EXPLANATIONS

OC MATHS TEST 7

1. d. A cube has 6 faces.
2. c. 5 cm × 2 = 10 cm. 10 cm × 4 = 40 cm (a square has 4 equal sides).
3. d.
4. b. 75% is the same as ¾. ¼ of 40 is 10 (it is the same as 40 ÷ 4). Therefore ¾ of 40 is 30 (10 × 3).
5. c. The shorter hand of the watch is the hours hand and the longer hand is the minutes hand.
6. a.
7. d. There are 12 eggs in a dozen, so 12 × 3 = 36.
8. b.
9. c.
10. a.
11. b. If a pie is cut into 8 even pieces, then each piece is $^1/_8$ of the pie. $^1/_8 + ^1/_8 = ^1/_4$
12. d. 9 ÷ 3 = 3. 3 + 2 = 5.

OC MATHS TEST 8

1. b.
2. d.
3. d. There are 3 five dollar notes, 1 twenty dollar note and 1 fifty dollar note. 3 × $5 = $15. $15 + $20 + $50 = $85.
4. b. There are 6 numbers on a dice and 3 are even numbers.
5. c. 36 hours is the same as 24 hours + 12 hours (a day and a half). A day and a half before 4:00 pm Monday is 4:00 am Sunday.
6. c. Each number is double the one before it.
7. b. There are 60 seconds in one minute and 30 seconds in half a minute. (4 × 60) + 30 = 240 + 30 = 270 seconds.
8. c. 6 + 7 = 13.
9. a. 15 – 6 = 9.
10. a. If Lucy can drive 40 kilometres in 1 hour, then she can drive 20 kilometres in half an hour (½ of 40 km = 20 km and ½ of 60 minutes = 30 minutes).

OC MATHS TEST 9

1. b.
2. d.
3. a.
4. d. 18 months is the same as 1 year and 6 months. One year after 5 May 1996 is 5 May 1997. 6 months later is 5 November 1997.
5. c. 15 + 3 – 4 = 14.
6. d. 3 × 4 – 5 = 7, and 13 – 9 × 1 = 4.
7. c.
8. d. $2.10 + $1.25 + $0.40 + $0.40 = $4.15. $5 – $4.15 = $0.85.
9. c. ¾ + 2 + ¼ = 3.
10. b. If there are 12 girls, there must be 21 boys (9 + 12 = 21). 21 boys + 12 girls = 33 students.
11. d. The multiple of the 2 outer numbers plus the inner number = the top number i.e. 7 × 7 + 5 = 54.
12. c.

ANSWERS AND EXPLANATIONS

OC MATHS TEST 10

1. b.
2. d.
3. a. 7 + 15 + 5 = 27.
4. d. 15 + 2 = 17.
5. d.
6. b. The numbers form the following pattern. 6 + 5 + 4 = 15 and 1 + 5 = 6. 1 + 5 = 6. 8 + 7 + 6 = 21 and 2 + 1 = 3.
7. b. 3 numbers on a dice are even. 3 + 1 = 4.
8. d. 2 + 7 = 9 and 2 × 7 = 14.
9. b. 10 + 1 + 1 = 12. 6 + 1 + 1 = 8. 12 + 12 + 8 + 8 = 24 + 16 = 40.
10. d.

OC MATHS TEST 11

1. a. 1 200 = 800 + 400 (½ of 800). Therefore it takes 5 minutes + 2.5 minutes (½ of 5 minutes).
2. a.
3. b. 6 × 2 = 12. ¼ of 12 = 3.
4. d.
5. d. 5 × 2 ½ = 10 + 2 ½ = 12 ½ kg. 15 - 12 ½ = 2 ½ kg.
6. c. 2 ½ + 2 ½ + 10 = 15 km.
7.b. 3:15 pm + 45 minutes = 4:00pm. 4:00 pm + 30 minutes + 20 minutes = 4:50 pm.
8. a.
9. a. 15 + 25 = 40.
10. d. 12 × 3 = 36. ½ × 12 = 6. 36 – 6 = 30.
11. a. Multiply the two bottom numbers then add the middle number to obtain the top number.

OC MATHS TEST 12

1. c. If the length is 12 cm, then the breadth is 6 cm. The area of the rectangle is 12 × 6 = 72 cm².
2. d.
3. a. 12 × 25 drops = 300 drops. 300 ÷ 100 = 3. 3 × 80 = 240 mL.
4. b.
5. c. Susannah receives 10, Lotte receives 10, Alix receives 5, and Marianne receives 20.
6. c.
7. a.
8. d.
9. b. 12 + 12 + 16 + 16 = 24 + 32 = 56 cm.
10. d. 4.5 × 60 minutes = 240 + 30 = 270 minutes
11. c.
12. c.

ANSWERS AND EXPLANATIONS

OC MATHS TEST 13

1. b.
2. d. 15 + 28 = 43 km.
3. d. There are 4 lots of 250 mL in 1000 L. 4 × 5 = 20.
4. c.
5. a. 80 + 70 + 70 + 35 + 40 + 130 + 100 = 525 m.
6. b. 525 m ÷ 5 = 105 m.
7. b. There are 20 squares in the rectangle, and 5 of those squares are shaded in i.e ¼ of the squares are shaded in.
8. d. 19 + 13 + 9 = 41.
9. a.
10. b.
11. d.

OC MATHS TEST 14

1. b.
2. c.
3. a.
4. d. 52 + 49 + 34 = 135 = 140 to the nearest 10.
5. c.
6. b.
7. a. 30 km ÷ 10 km = 3. 120 minutes ÷ 3 = 40 minutes.
8. d.
9. b.
10. d.
11. b.

OC MATHS TEST 15

1. d. The previous two numbers are added together and then doubled.
2. d.
3. b. 29 + 37 + 15 = 81. 100 − 81 = 19%.
4. a. 100 − 29 = 71%
5. d.
6. a.
7. a.
8. b.
9. d. $5.00 ÷ 2 = $2.50. $10.50 ÷ 5 = $2.10. Therefore the box of 5 tangelos for $10.50 is the best deal.
10. a.

OC MATHS TEST 16

1. c. 18 + 18 + 9 = 45 litres.
2. b.
3. d. 15 oranges + 18 apples + 12 pears = 45 pieces of fruit.
4. d. 18 − 12 = 6.
5. c.
6. a. 3 ½ × $5.50 = $17.50 (3 ½ × $5) + $1.75 (3 ½ × $0.50) = $19.25.
7. c.
8. a.
9. c. Each number is divided by three and then one is added to the result. 48 ÷ 3 + 1 = 17
10. c. 700 ÷ 9 is closest to 78.

ANSWERS AND EXPLANATIONS

OC MATHS EXTENSION

1. d. The pattern is 8^2, 7^2, 6^2, 5^2...

2. d. $32 \div 4 = 8$. $8 - 3 = 5$ chairs in Jonathan's dining room. Therefore Helen has 10 chairs in her dining room.

3. b.

4. d.

5. b. $\$13.95 \times 2 + \$18 = \$45.90$. $\$45.90 + \$4.50$ ($\$18 \div 4$) $= \$50.40$. $\$60.00 - \$50.40 = \$9.60$.

6. a.

7. a.

8. c.

9. d. This question is related to the numerical placement of letters in the alphabet. So M is the 13th letter in the alphabet, E is the 5th, Y is the 25th etc.

ME + YOU = 135 + 251521 = 251656 = BEAFEF

UP + OUT = 2116 + 152120 = 154236= AEDBCF

IN + ON = 914 + 1514 = 2428 = BDBH

10. c. Blake empties 1 Litre of water every 20 seconds. $20 \times 20 = 400$ seconds = 6 minutes 40 seconds. However, as Blake starts emptying the first cup of water at 0 seconds, 5 seconds must be subtracted from the final answer. Thus the most correct answer is 6 minutes 35 seconds.

11. a. $17 \times 20 = 340$ seconds. 340 seconds – 5 seconds = 5 minutes 35 seconds.

12. c. 24 + 12 + 260 = 296 legs.

13. d. $7 \times 700 = 4\,900$. $3 \times 550 = 1\,650$. $1\,650 + 4\,900 = 6\,550$. $2 \times 6\,550 = 13\,100$ grams.

14. b. $5 \times 5 \times 5 = 125$ cm³. $20 \times 10 \times 10 = 2\,000$ cm³. $2\,000 \div 125 = 16$.

15. b. 20 + 20 + 20 + 30 + 30 + 15 = 135.

CORRECTIONS

CORRECTIONS

CORRECTIONS